I0196345

Magical Musical Kingdom
Song Book

Frances Turnbull

Copyright © 2016 Frances Turnbull

Magical Musical Kingdom Song Book
All rights reserved
Musicaliti Publishing, Bolton, UK

ISBN: 978-1907935770

SONG LIST

Bonus Songs

Ukulele Chords

Ukuleles are small, accessible and relatively cheap instruments that can be used to play the accompaniment to many songs.

Each string should be tuned to specific notes (can be found on tuned instruments like xylophones, pianos or recorders etc.). The standard ukulele tuning is:

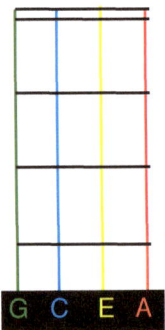 

G C E A

God Can't Eat Ants

By placing your fingers on the frets at the positions on the pictures, (between the lines), you change the sound of the strings into chords when strummed altogether.

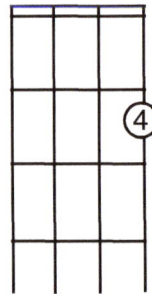

C

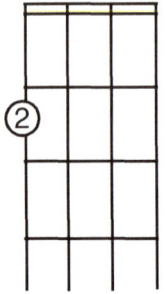

Am

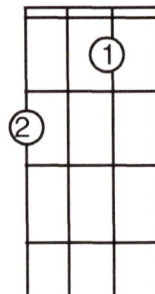

F

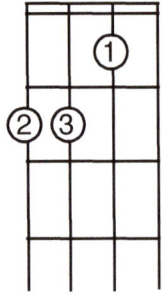

Dm

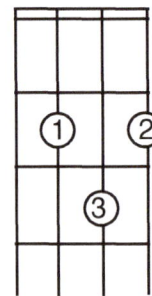

G

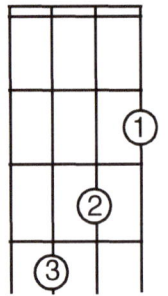

Em

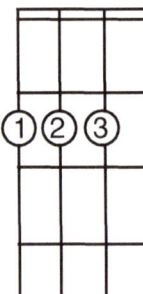

D

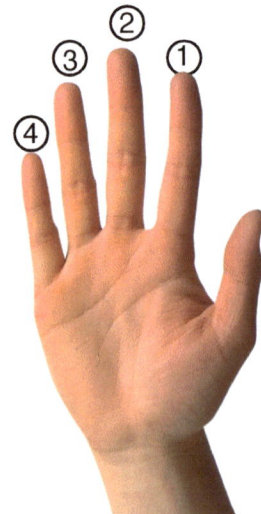

usicaliti

usicali

A long time ago in a magical, musical kingdom far, far away …

A long time ago in a magical musical kingdom far, far away, there lived King Crotchet.

King Crotchet was big and strong, and when he walked past, everyone stopped to watch him because he was so loud and took such big steps.

King Crotchet ruled wisely and justly and had a great crown full of every precious stone in the world.

People loved King Crotchet so much that they travelled far and wide to find the most precious stone and every week, he would choose the best new precious stones to add to his crown.

The rest of the precious stones were added to the walls of his magnificent castle that shone each morning on the magical hill.

Every day King Crotchet loved to play croquet, a game where he would hit balls though hoops in the ground.

I am King

Arranged by F. Turnbull

Written by F. Turnbull

C   Am

I am King and I am best in

C   Am

North and South and East and West - land.

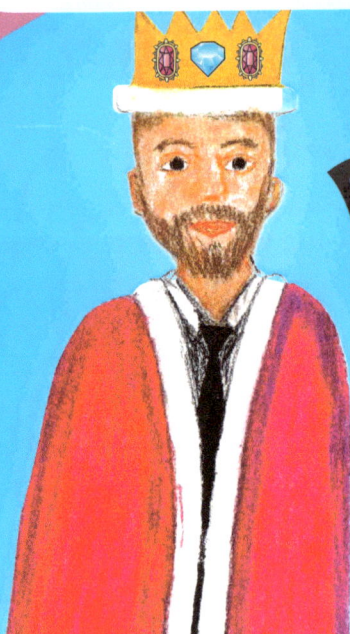

Old King Glory

Arranged by F Turnbull

Traditional

C   G

Old King Glo - ry on the moun - tain, the moun - tain was so high, it

C

al - most touched the sky, and it's one, two, three, fol - low me!

Queens are Royal

Arranged by F. Turnbull

Written by F. Turnbull

C

Queens are ro - yal, queens are grand, and they love their coun - try land.

Am C

Where they go the wa - ters gli - sten, they say this to all who li - sten.

The Queen of Hearts

Arranged by F Turnbull

Traditional

C

The Queen of Hearts, she made some tarts all on a sum - mer's day,

Am

The Knave of Hearts, he stole those tarts and took them all a - way.

C

The King of Hearts called for the tarts and beat the Knave full sore,

Am C

The Knave of Hearts brought back the tarts and vowed he'd steal no more.

A long time ago in a magical musical kingdom far, far away, there lived King Crotchet, married to Queen Quaver.

Queen Quaver moved quickly and quietly, and was always two steps ahead of the King.

Queen Quaver was very beautiful, the most beautiful lady in the land, and people travelled from all over the world to see her.

Wherever she went, the mountains peaked higher, the grass shone greener, the flowers grew brighter and even the rivers shone until they glistened, although she hardly made a sound.

Queen Quaver loved to play tennis and would always bounce and hit the ball as quickly as she could.

A long time ago in a magical musical kingdom far, far away, there lived King Crotchet, married to Queen Quaver, protected by brave and handsome Knight Quaver-Crotchet.

Knight Quaver-Crotchet was the most brave person in all the land and would do anything to protect his King Crotchet and Queen Quaver.

When bad people took things from the King, Knight Quaver-Crotchet would travel to the other side of the world and never give up until they were caught.

He was not scared of anything or anyone because he was fit and well trained.

When he was training, Knight Quaver-Crotchet loved to fence, a sport with swords that relied on cunning and expertise.

Knight and Horse

Arranged by F. Turnbull

Written by F. Turnbull

Knight and horse ride fier - cely, fier - cely,

Knight and horse move quick - ly quick - ly.

Ne - ver ti - ring, bra - vely, bra - vely,

Save King and slay beas - tie, beas - tie.

Grand Old Duke of York

C   G

Oh, the grand old duke of York, he had ten thou - sand men, he

C   F   C

marched them up to the top of the hill and he marched them down a - again. And

C   G

when they were up, they were up, and when they were down, they were

C   F   C   G   C

down, and when they were on - ly half - way up they were nei - ther up nor down.

Pink Hat Lady

Arranged by F. Turnbull

Written by F. Turnbull

Pink hat, pink shoes, posh frock, read news,

nod and sip tea, lift hat, curt - sey.

Down Came My Friend

Arranged by F. Turnbull

Traditional

Down came my friend and down came two,

down came two friends and they were dressed in blue.

musicaliti

A long time ago in a magical musical kingdom far away, there lived King Crotchet, married to Queen Quaver, protected by brave and handsome Knight Quaver-Crotchet, married to Lady Minim who looked after the animals.

Lady Minim was a very special Lady who was very good at caring for sick animals.

Lady Minim moved slowly and calmly so that they were never startled or afraid and some people said she could even speak the secret language of animals.

When she was not caring for animals, Lady Minim loved to play bowls, gently rolling one ball to hit the bull's eye.

A long time ago in a magical musical kingdom far, far away, there lived King Crotchet, married to Queen Quaver, protected by brave and handsome Knight Quaver-Crotchet, married to Lady Minim who looked after the animals, and lived together with Princess Semiquaver.

Princess Semiquaver was the King's most precious jewel, his only daughter.

Semiquaver moved even more quickly than the Queen and was often seen running quickly or spinning in fields, forests and near ponds with all the animals of the Kingdom.

She would start by moving very quietly she got louder and louder as she got further away from the Castle.

One day when she was at the pond, she saw a little frog.

He had a beautiful golden head and she thought he looked like a little prince so she called him Frog Prince.

Princess Semiquaver

Arranged by F. Turnbull

Written by F. Turnbull

Cir - cle to the left, Se - mi - qua - ver,

Cir - cle to the left Se - mi - qua - ver,

Cir - cle to the left, Se - mi - qua - ver,

You're the one my dar - ling.

Built my Princess

Arranged by F Turnbull

Traditional

C

Am

Built my Prin-cess a fine brick house, Built it in a gar - den, I

C

Am

C

put her in but she jumped out so fare thee we-ll my dar - lin'.

Hopping Hopping

Arranged by F. Turnbull

Written by F. Turnbull

Hop-ping hop-ping on a log, I'm a hop-ping lit - tle frog.

Kiss, kiss, kiss, now I am a prince!

The Little Bells

Arranged by F Turnbull

Traditional

The lit - tle bells of West-min-ster go ding dong, ding dong dong.

A long time ago in a magical musical kingdom far, far away, there lived King Crotchet, married to Queen Quaver, protected by brave and handsome Knight Quaver-Crotchet, married to Lady Minim who looked after the animals, and lived together with Princess Semiquaver and Frog Prince.

Frog Prince saw Princess Semiquaver every day with a juicy bug snack and one day, Frog Prince did a froggy somersault trick.

Semiquaver laughed out loud, and thought he was so clever that she gave him a kiss.

Poof! Suddenly the frog disappeared and a handsome prince appeared in his place, from a spell that a naughty elf put on him.

He loved his new name so much that even as a person, he wanted to be called Frog Prince!

Although he used to croak very loudly, he was so glad that he could now speak quietly.

His favourite sport used to be horse riding and now that he was a person again, Frog Prince could ride his horse again, too.

A long time ago in a magical musical kingdom far, far away, there lived King Crotchet, married to Queen Quaver, protected by brave and handsome Knight Quaver-Crotchet, married to Lady Minim who looked after the animals, and lived together with Princess Semiquaver and Frog Prince, near naughty Elfen.

But far away from the Magical Kingdom, in a dark and dreary cave full of broken instruments lived Elfen, the naughty, creeping elf who turned Frog Prince into a frog.

He did not like musical instruments, only the sound of voices, and when he was cross he crept around and broke all the instruments he could find.

Elfen was very cross with Princess Semiquaver for changing Frog Prince back so he did another magic spell and crept into the castle and put her in a secret tower, far away from her family.

Princess Semiquaver was very sad and King Crotchet and Frog Prince were furious.

Queen Quaver and Lady Minim asked Knight Quaver-Crotchet to please find her so Knight Quaver-Crotchet left immediately to search every tower in the land to find Princess Semiquaver.

Elfen

Arranged by F. Turnbull

Written by F. Turnbull

El - fen, el - fen, cree ping, snea king, caught the prin cess, now in hi - ding.

Elfen Protector

Arranged by F Turnbull

Traditional

Elf - en Pro - tec - tor was dressed in all green,
Elf - fen Pro - tec - tor was sent to the Queen, The
Queen did not like him, no more did the King, so
El - fen Pro - tec - tor was sent back a - gain.

Skipping Flying Fairy

Arranged by F. Turnbull

Written by F. Turnbull

Skip - ping, fly - ing, o - ver the woods,

El - fen's gold, he's up - to no good,

Skip - ping, fly - ing way up high,

Hang gold on a moon - beam high.

Love Somebody

Arranged by F Turnbull

Traditional

Love some-bo - dy, yes I do, Love some-bo-dy, yes I do,

Love some-bo - dy, yes, I do, Love some-bo-dy but I won't say who

Love some-bo - dy, yes I do, Love some-bo-dy, yes I do,

Love some-bo - dy, yes, I do, Love some-bo-dy and it's you, you, you.

A long time ago in a magical musical kingdom far, far away, there lived King Crotchet, married to Queen Quaver, protected by brave and handsome Knight Quaver-Crotchet, married to Lady Minim who looked after the animals, and lived together with Princess Semiquaver and Frog Prince, near naughty Elfen and Flying Fairy.

Flying Fairy met Knight Quaver-Crotchet while he was searching every tower in the land, as she flew here and there.

Knight Quaver-Crotchet searched Flying Fairy's tower, but Princess Semiquaver just was not there.

When he told Flying Fairy what Elfen had done and how sad Frog Prince was, Flying Fairy got very cross indeed.

She never spoke, but played music because she was surrounded by every instrument in the world.

She wanted to play a trick on Elfen so using her special magic, she flew to his dark cave and saw all the broken instruments.

Right at the back of the cave was a very shiny pot of gold, hidden behind the instruments.

Flying Fairy picked it up and flew right to the moon and hung it on a moon beam as punishment!

A long time ago in a magical musical kingdom far, far away, there lived King Crotchet, married to Queen Quaver, protected by the brave and handsome Knight Quaver-Crotchet, who was married to Lady Minim who looked after the animals, and lived together with Princess Semiquaver and Frog Prince, near naughty Elfen and Flying Fairy, and far away from Dragon Semibreve.

Dragon Semibreve had a lair with a castle on the farthest point of the Magical Musical Kingdom.

As Knight Quaver-Crotchet got further and further away from the Kingdom, he could not even see the castle as he got nearer and nearer to Dragon Semibreve's lair.

Everything Dragon Semibreve did was slow because she was so big.

She opened her eyes slowly, she walked slowly and even blew fire out slowly.

When Dragon Semibreve blew fire out, everything would start shaking altogether, her arms and legs, tummy and tail, until she stopped.

Dragon Semibreve did not like things that moved fast, so when Elfen took Princess Semibreve to the tower, they had to creep slowly and quietly.

Knight Quaver-Crotchet arrived just in time to see the naughty elf and the princess sneaking, and he wanted to save her quickly.

Moving quickly, Knight Quaver-Crotchet suddenly felt like he was flying as Dragon Semibreve caught him.

Before he knew what had happened, Knight Quaver-Crotchet was trapped in the tower with Princess Semiquaver and Elfen.

Dragon

Arranged by F. Turnbull

Written by F. Turnbull

C   Am

Dra - gon breathe fire, dra - gon, stomp loud,

C   Am   C

dra - gon take her In the to - wer.

Do, Do, Pity my Case

Arranged by F Turnbull

Traditional

C

Do, do, pi - ty my case, In some Dra - gon's gar - den, My

Am   C

clothes to wash when I get ho - me, In some Dra - gon's gar - den.

Beautiful Unicorn

Arranged by F. Turnbull

Written by F. Turnbull

Beau-ti-ful u-ni-corn, where do you hide, In the val-ley.

Beau-ti-ful u-ni-corn, let's take a ride! Save the fam'-ly.

The Dragon and the Unicorn

Arranged by F Turnbull

Traditional

The dra-gon and the u-ni-corn were figh-ting for the

crown, The dra-gon beat the u-ni-corn all a-round the

town. Some gave them white bread, some gave them brown,

some gave them plum-cake and drummed them out of town

A long time ago in a magical musical kingdom far, far away, there lived King Crotchet, married to Queen Quaver, protected by the brave and handsome Knight Quaver-Crotchet, who was married to Lady Minim who looked after the animals, and lived together with Princess Semiquaver and Frog Prince, near naughty Elfen and Flying Fairy, and far away from Dragon Semibreve and Unicorn Triplet.

The dreadful news of the capture of Knight-Quaver-Crotchet, Princess Semiquaver and Elfen travelled over the Magical Musical Kingdom until a dancing Unicorn, alone in a field, heard the sad tale.

He always played on his own, dancing every single day, but when he heard the news, Unicorn Triplet's horn began to glow, which meant he was very, very cross.

Shaking out his golden wings, he flew straight to Dragon Semibreve's tower and very quickly, Knight Quaver-Crotchet and Princess Semiquaver jumped on his back.

Elfen took so long to creep to the window that he could only hold onto Unicorn's tail, as they flew through the fiery mountains and back to the castle.

King Crotchet was so pleased to have his Magical Musical Kingdom restored that he threw a huge party.

There was so much music that Elfen crept away back to his cave and sometimes, when the sky is right, you can see that the moon still looks a little golden, where Flying Fairy hung Elfen's gold on the moonbeam.

Twinkle twinkle

Traditional

Twin - kle,   twin - kle   lit - tle   star,   how   I   won - der   what   you   are,
Up   a - bove   the   world   so   high,   like   a   dia - mond   in   the   sky,   twin - kle,   twin - kle
lit - tle   star,   how   I   won - der   what   you   are.

BONUS SONGS

Row Row Row your boat

Traditional

Arranged by Frances Turnbull

Row,   row,   row   your   boat   gent - ly   down   the   stream,
mer - ri - ly,   mer - ri - ly,   mer - ri - ly,   mer - ri - ly,   life   is   but   a   dream.

My Song: _____

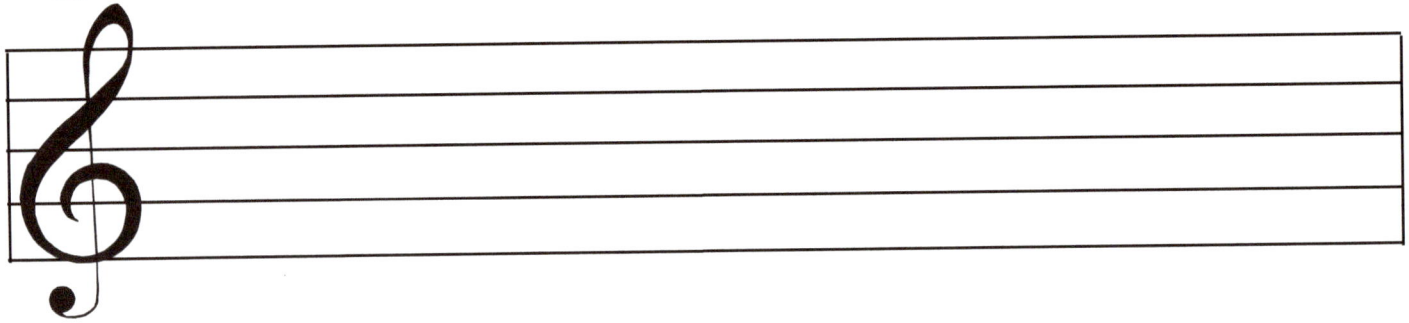

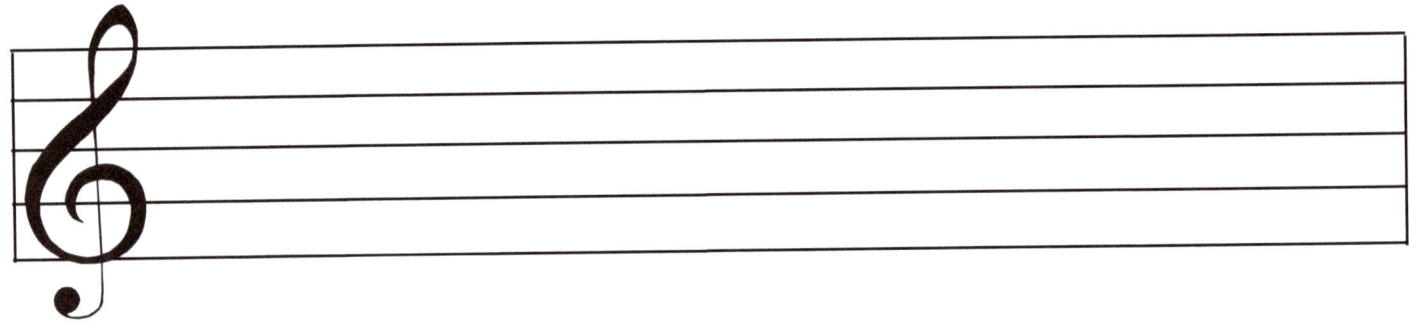

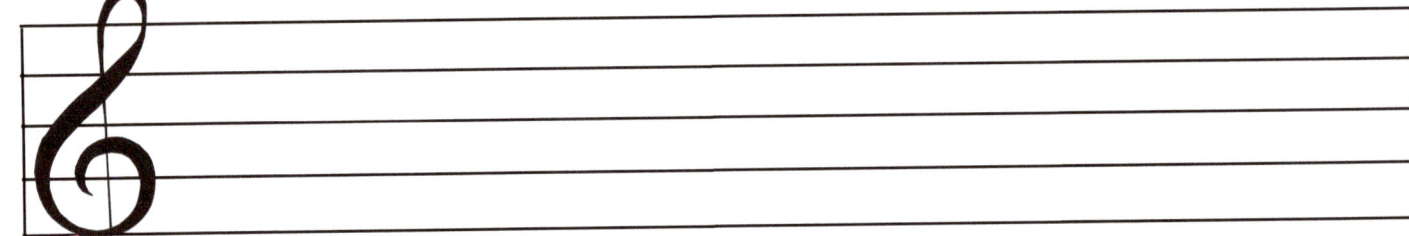

The End

Have you seen our other books?

Music Gone Wild Song Book:
Animal Songs for Ukulele
ISBN 9781907935688

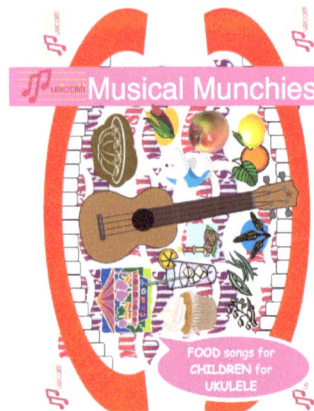

Musical Munchies Song Book:
Food Songs for Ukulele
TBC

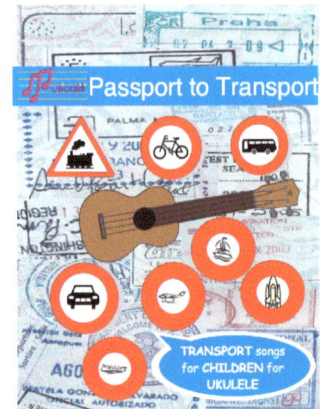

Passport to Transport Song Book:
Transport Songs for Ukulele
TBC

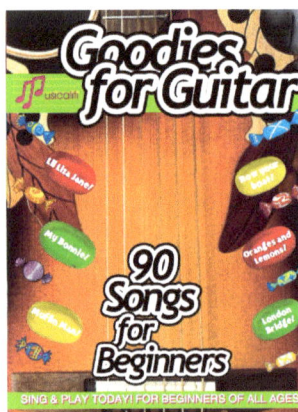

Goodies for Guitar:
90 songs for beginners
ISBN 9781907935695

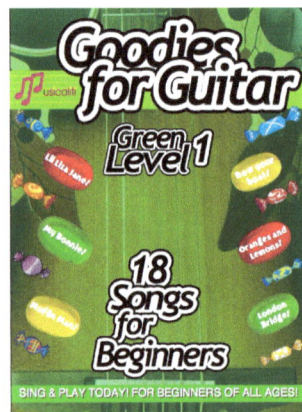

Goodies for Guitar: Lvl 1
18 songs for beginners
ISBN 9781907935701

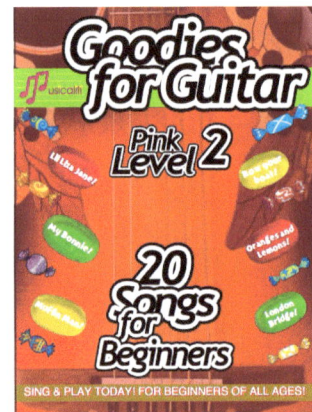

Goodies for Guitar: Lvl 2
20 songs for beginners
ISBN 9781907935718

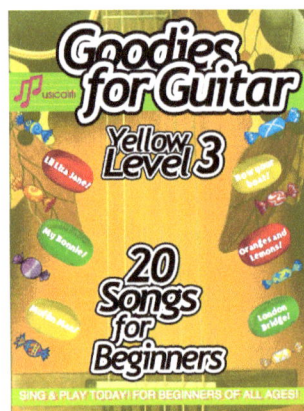

Goodies for Guitar: Lvl 3
20 songs for beginners
ISBN 9781907935725

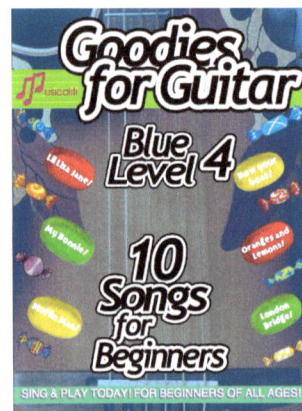

Goodies for Guitar: Lvl 4
10 songs for beginners
ISBN 9781907935732

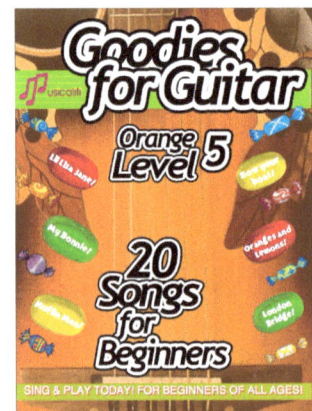

Goodies for Guitar: Lvl 5
20 songs for beginners
ISBN 9781907935749

FIND US ON:

www.ingramcontent.com/pod-product-compliance
Lightning Source LLC
Chambersburg PA
CBHW042124040426
42450CB00002B/58